PRE-COLUMBIAN ART

in the

Denver Art Museum Collection

Margaret Young-Sánchez

PRE-COLUMBIAN ART

in the

Denver Art Museum Collection

Frederick and Jan Mayer Center
for Pre-Columbian and Spanish Colonial Art
at the Denver Art Museum

Design and maps by Michael Raeburn, Cacklegoose Press

Printed and bound in Italy by Litografica Faenza Group

Museum photography by William J. O'Connor, except for figures 6 and 35, by Jeff Wells, and figure 5, by Eric Stephenson

ISBN 0-914738-47-X

Library of Congress Control Number: 2003108617

Cover illustrations: (front) **Detail of a Paracas mantle** (figure 28); *(back)* **Moche portrait jar** (figure 32), **Chimú-Inca ear ornament** (figure 39), **Teotihuacán mask** (figure 12).
Half-title illustration: **Conte-style breastplate** (figure 23).
Frontispiece: **La Selva-style warrior figure with trophy head** (figure 18).

Dimensions are given as height × width × depth (or height × diameter).

To Denver's extraordinary philanthropists Jan and Frederick R. Mayer,
with gratitude and admiration

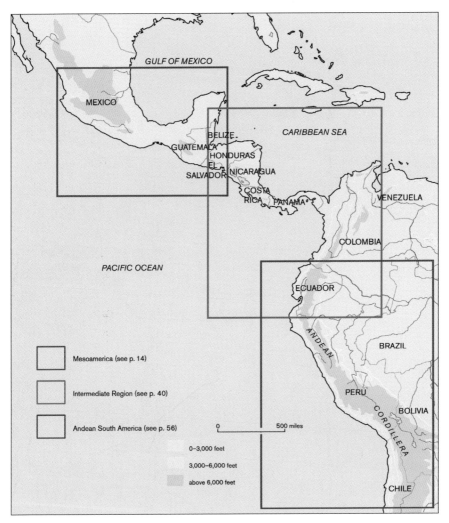

GULF OF MEXICO

MEXICO

CARIBBEAN SEA

BELIZE
GUATEMALA
HONDURAS
EL
SALVADOR NICARAGUA
COSTA
RICA PANAMA

VENEZUELA

COLOMBIA

PACIFIC OCEAN

ECUADOR

A N D E A N

BRAZIL

PERU

BOLIVIA

C O R D I L L E R A

CHILE

Mesoamerica (see p. 14)

Intermediate Region (see p. 40)

Andean South America (see p. 56)

0   500 miles

0–3,000 feet

3,000–6,000 feet

above 6,000 feet

*Map of Mexico, Central America, and Andean South America,
showing the three principal regions of pre-Columbian cultures with
modern national boundaries.*

Contents

Preface

The Denver Art Museum's collection of pre-Columbian art (currently numbering more than five thousand objects) is one of the institution's most important assets. Although the first object was acquired in 1951, sustained collecting did not begin until the 1960s. Robert Stroessner, the charismatic curator who joined the museum in 1966 and led the New World department until his untimely death in 1991, parlayed limited financial resources and boundless enthusiasm into one of the finest, most comprehensive pre-Columbian collections in the United States. His supporters in this endeavor included patrons from Denver and beyond—Mr. and Mrs. Horace E. Day, Mr. and Mrs. Lindsay A. Duff, Mr. Douglas R. Hurlburt, Mrs. Lewis K. Land, Mr. William I. Lee, Mr. and Mrs. Morris A. Long, Mr. and Mrs. Edward L. Luben, Mr. and Mrs. Cedric H. Marks, Mr. and Mrs. Raphael J. Moses, Dr. and Mrs. M. Larry Ottis, Mr. and Mrs. Robert H. Power, and Mr. and Mrs. Edward T. Strauss, to name just a few. Bob's greatest supporters were Jan and Frederick R. Mayer, who provided funds for numerous acquisitions and donated much of their personal collection of pre-Columbian art from Costa Rica. (The Mayers also provide crucial moral and financial support for building the Denver Art Museum's collection of Spanish Colonial art, generally acknowledged as the most important in the United States.)

Pre-Columbian art at the museum includes several areas of special strength. The Costa Rican collection is encyclopedic, with extensive, aesthetically outstanding holdings of stone sculpture, jade, gold, and ceramics. Maya ceramics are also exceptional: rare pre-Classic vessels and figurines, Early Classic cache vessels and blackware, and Late Classic painted cylinders

Facing page: **Detail of a feline head on an Inca jug from Peru** (figure 38).

9

and modeled figurines are all included. Teotihuacán and West Mexican ceramic traditions (especially Nayarit and Colima) are also well represented. The especially choice collections of Wari and Tiwanaku art from South America reflect the academic interests of curators Gordon McEwan (1991–1998) and Margaret Young-Sánchez (1999 to present). Growth of the pre-Columbian collection continues through both purchases and gifts. Research, publications, and public programs seek to make this valuable resource better known to the Denver public and also to the national and international audience of pre-Columbian art lovers and scholars.

I gratefully acknowledge the contributions and encouragement of my colleagues Donna Pierce, Gretchen DeSciose, Julie Wilson, and Anne Tennant. Christine Deal played an active role in all phases of this book's preparation and deserves my special thanks. My husband, Fernando Sánchez, and I have made numerous visits to Latin America together. Many of his photographs of archaeological sites and monuments are illustrated here. Armand Labbé kindly supplied two photographs from San Agustín, Colombia. Bill O'Connor photographed the Denver Art Museum objects, aided by Carole Lee, John Lupe, Mark Knobelsdorf, and Doug Wagner. Conservators Jessica Fletcher and Carl Patterson examined and treated several pieces. Michael Raeburn edited the text, created maps, and designed the book, with crucial assistance from Laura Caruso and Lisa Levinson in the museum's publications department. Director Lewis Sharp and patrons Jan and Frederick R. Mayer provided both inspiration and the moral and financial support that brought this project to fruition.

Introduction

Archaeologists still seek to determine when human beings first arrived in the Americas—some believe it was as many as forty thousand years ago. Little art was produced, however, until a few thousand years ago, when settled life began and populations increased. Agriculture and intensive marine exploitation supported the development of civilization in Mexico and Central America, and in Peru. These civilizations built great cities and systems of communication and transportation, developed bodies of science and literature, and created a series of magnificent artistic traditions. Today, these civilizations are known as pre-Columbian, which means simply "before Columbus." While Columbus's arrival in the Americas did little, by itself, to change New World history, it ushered in an era of European exploration and conquest that profoundly affected all Native American peoples. New languages, religions, technologies, domesticated animals, and crops were introduced—sometimes imposed by force, sometimes willingly adopted. New diseases were also introduced, with devastating consequences for native societies.

This book focuses on three major culture-regions in what is now Latin America. Each region is defined by cultural traits that link its peoples together and distinguish them from their neighbors. The northernmost culture-region is Mesoamerica, which extends roughly from central Mexico through Belize, Guatemala, Honduras, and part of El Salvador. The Intermediate Region encompasses southern Central America and northern South America, including Nicaragua, Costa Rica, Panama, and Colombia. Andean South America, the third culture-region, parallels the Andean Cordillera and includes the modern nations of Ecuador, Peru, Bolivia, and Chile. The Denver Art Museum contains one of the most comprehensive collections of pre-Columbian art in the world, with extensive holdings from all three culture-regions. Although only a few examples can be illustrated here, most of the collection is on permanent exhibition and accessible to visitors.

Mesoamerica

THE OLMEC

Mesoamerica is defined by a constellation of cultural traits, including: agriculture and diet based on a triad of crops (maize, beans, squash), the use of a 365-day solar calendar and a 260-day ritual calendar, the playing of a sacred ballgame, the construction of monumental public architecture, and a religion that emphasized blood sacrifice. Mesoamerica's first civilization to embody all or most of these traits was the Olmec. Olmec sites are concentrated in the warm, humid Gulf Coast region of Mexico, although Olmec architecture, sculpture, and cave paintings are also found in central Mexico.

San Lorenzo, located in the state of Veracruz on the southern Gulf Coast, is one of the earliest known Olmec sites (about 1200–900 BC). Monumental architecture at the site includes a large earthen mound, perhaps built in the form of a bird with outspread wings. At La Venta, in Tabasco, the Olmec built a radial pyramid and rectangular earthen mounds. At both sites, large blocks of basalt, transported from the Tuxtla Mountains about eighty miles away, were carved to form components of water control and drainage systems, as well as large-scale sculptures.

Most famous are huge heads, believed to portray Olmec rulers, and large blocks called altars that are now believed to have served as thrones. These show a male figure emerging from a niche that appears to represent a cave or opening in the earth. On the lap of some of these figures lies an infant-like supernatural being. It is thought that the rulers of Olmec sites served as mediators between the people and the spiritual forces of nature. The ruler was thus responsible for maintaining abundance and well-being for the community. The emphasis in Olmec art on the physical appearance of

---

Facing page: **Detail of the head of a ruler on a Maya panel** (figure 5).

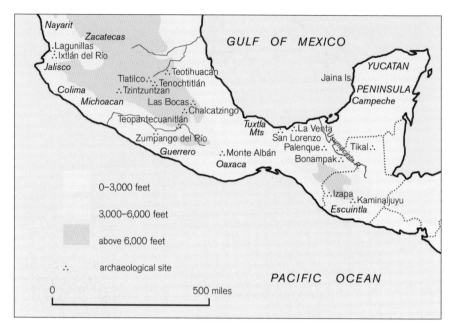

rulers (rather than on elaborate costume or accouterments) suggests that power derived from individual charisma rather than from the office itself.

In addition to large-scale works in stone, the Olmec produced masterful small-scale sculpture in jade and ceramic. The Olmec prized jade and other green stones (a trait shared by all later Mesoamerican peoples) and probably traveled great distances to obtain it. From jade they fabricated celts (axes), figurines, masks, and ornaments. The faces on Olmec figurines are distinctive, with heavy eyelids and thick lips with downturned corners. Some are jaguarlike, with snarling or crying mouths. Called were-jaguars (like werewolves), these figurines suggest possible shamanic transformation of humans into animals.

Figure 1 shows an extraordinary example of Olmec sculpture in ceramic. Like most Olmec sculptures, the figure is sexless. The limbs are smooth, rounded forms that in no way reflect the anatomical reality of bones and muscle. The delicately modeled oval face has slitlike, slanted eyes and the characteristically Olmec downturned mouth. This sculpture was reportedly discovered in the state of Guerrero in central Mexico. The Olmec established a presence in this region through trade, pilgrimage, or possibly warfare. Sites like Chalcatzingo in Morelos and Teopantecuanitlán in Guerrero were probably constructed by the Olmec.

Contemporary peoples living in central Mexico and as far south as Costa Rica prized Olmec art, which must have carried cultural prestige and perhaps religious meaning. Olmec-style ceramics have been discovered among

1. **Seated Figure. Olmec. About 1000–500 BC.** Zumpango del Río, Guerrero, Mexico. Earthenware with slip, pigments, 14″ × 12½″ × 9¼″. Funds from various donors; 1975.50.
This hand-modeled hollow figure is covered with a cream-colored clay slip that has been carefully burnished to produce a smooth, glossy finish. All pre-Columbian ceramics are earthenware—fired at a temperature below 1000° C.

grave offerings at Tlatilco (in the state of Mexico) and Las Bocas (in Puebla). Most grave goods at such sites are local in style, however. A clay figurine (figure 2), which dates between 1200 and 900 BC, radiates grace and vitality. Like most such figurines from central Mexico, this one is female and scantily clad, with voluptuously full hips and thighs, high breasts, and a narrow waist. Hands and feet are small and delicate. The round head is carefully modeled, with earspools and a caplike coiffure. Such idealized depictions of women may have been used in household rites to promote health and fertility.

2. Female Figurine. Las Bocas, Puebla (?), Mexico. About 1200–900 BC. Earthenware with pigment, 7⅛″ × 2¾″ × 1¾″. Department acquisition funds; 1983.116.
Ceramic figurines were manufactured by a variety of cultures throughout Mesoamerican prehistory. The predominance of nubile or pregnant females suggests the crucial importance of human fertility in the continuity and prosperity of society.

Monte Albán, Oaxaca, Mexico. View south from the North Mound
(photo by Fernando Sánchez).

THE ZAPOTECS

The Zapotec people of the Valley of Oaxaca were also contemporaries of
the Olmec, and early Zapotec art reflects Olmec stylistic influence. The
Zapotecs continue to live in Oaxaca today, demonstrating at least three
thousand years of cultural continuity. The most important Zapotec site,
Monte Albán, was occupied from approximately 500 BC to AD 900 and
functioned as the capital of the entire region. Built on the artificially
leveled summit of a hill, the site offered views of all three branches of
the Valley of Oaxaca. Monte Albán's architecture, constructed of stone,
includes palaces, temples (which may have also fulfilled administrative
purposes), a ball court, and an unusual arrow-shaped structure perhaps
associated with astronomical observations.

The most famous and characteristic form of Zapotec art is gray ceramic
vessels that were buried with the dead as funerary offerings. The gray color

3. Double-Chambered Vessel. Zapotec. About 150 BC–AD 200.
Oaxaca, Mexico. Earthenware, 6″ × 4¼″ × 4½″. Gift of William I.
Lee; 1985.651.
This vessel depicts a figure using a tumpline across the forehead to lift a
heavy load. No beasts of burden are native to Mesoamerica, so goods
were commonly transported in canoes or on human backs.

was produced by smothering the fire after it reached a temperature suf-
ficient to harden and strengthen the clay. This process creates a low-oxygen
(reduction) atmosphere, which drives carbon into the surface of the ceramics, turning them gray. Early Zapotec ceramics (figure 3) were hand built,
with simple, smoothly curved forms. Delicate carving and incision were
employed to articulate forms and delineate facial features and costume elements. Later Zapotec ceramics (about AD 600–900), called effigy urns,
were standardized. Their construction began with a vertical cylinder, closed
at the bottom. Flat slabs of clay were cut, shaped, and attached to the front
of the cylinder to form a human body, usually in seated pose. While the
body and face are simple, the headdress and ornaments are extremely

ornate, built with layers of elements cut from slabs of clay. The headdress ornaments were symbolic and served to identify the deity or individual portrayed and indicate his or her attributes. Flowers, bats, butterflies, and glyphs were all included. The glyphs (often calendar dates) may indicate birth dates, which were highly meaningful to most Mesoamerican peoples.

The Izapa Style and the Maya

A large region in southern Mesoamerica (southern Mexico, Guatemala, Belize, and parts of Honduras and El Salvador) is now inhabited by Maya peoples. About 100 BC–AD 100, several centuries after the decline of Olmec civilization, a style developed in the Pacific lowlands of Guatemala that is now known as Izapa (named after a site where artifacts in this style were recovered). Relatively little is known about Izapa culture, although its art is considered ancestral to the later Maya style. Izapa-style stelae (low-relief carvings on upright stone slabs or blocks) depict elaborately costumed rulers, deities, and ancestors. Small-scale art objects are rare. An extraordinary example in the collection is a cylindrical stone cup (figure 4) carved

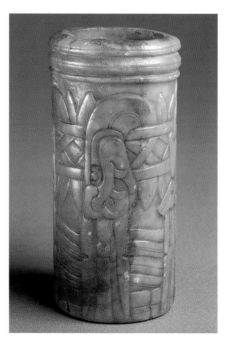

4. Cylindrical Container. Izapa.
About 100 BC–AD 100. Guatemala.
Jade, 4½″ × 2⅛″ (diameter).
Gift of Walt Disney Imagineering and Florence R. and Ralph L. Burgess Trust; 1987.204.
Jade and other green stones were prized by all Mesoamerican cultures, who associated the color with growth and fertility. Hollow drills, string, stone tools, and grit were employed to painstakingly shape and decorate objects made of this precious material.

with low-relief serpents, plaited bands, and strips of cloth or perhaps liquid. In later Maya thought, snakes were associated with the earth and running water but also with the sky, which was often depicted as a great, double-headed serpent. Plaited mats were symbols of royalty.

The ancient Maya were never united into a single political unit, but instead formed numerous competitive kingdoms, each with a royal court. The largest and most powerful Maya cities dominated their smaller neighbors, which were ruled by lesser noble lineages. Important public structures like temples, palaces, and ball courts were built with stone and plaster and often decorated with relief sculpture.

The Maya developed the most complex and sophisticated writing system in all the Americas. With it, they could record dates thousands of years in the past and perform the mathematical calculations necessary for predicting astronomical events like eclipses and the appearances and disappearances of Venus. The Maya also recorded both mythological and historical events. Portraits of rulers were carved on stone stelae (freestanding slabs) and monuments, accompanied by inscriptions detailing their lineages, dates of birth, accession to rule, conquests, and ritual performances. The low-relief limestone panel in figure 5 portrays the ruler of an as-yet-unknown Maya site probably located in the Usumacinta-Petexbatun River region of Mexico or Guatemala. Depicted in profile, he wears a jaguar headdress with long quetzal feather plumes, a cape decorated with human eyeballs, and high-backed sandals. Precious jade jewelry is worn at the forehead, ears, chest, and wrists. The ruler performs a ritual, scattering incense with his right hand from the bag he carries.

The Maya also developed one of the ancient world's greatest painting traditions. Large-scale narrative scenes were painted in brilliant mineral pigments on the interior walls of buildings. The most famous example is found at Bonampak in Chiapas, Mexico. Recorded in the murals there are a battle scene, the arraignment of prisoners, and a celebration—seemingly to honor the designation of a royal heir. More common than murals are polychrome painted ceramics. Unfired vessel surfaces were usually covered with white or orange slip (finely ground clay suspended in water). This

5. Panel. Maya. About AD 780. Mexico or Guatemala. Limestone,
79″ × 46″. Department acquisition funds; 1997.149a–g.
Low-relief stone sculptures occupied both public and private spaces at
ancient Maya courts. This well-preserved panel probably comes from a
palace and portrays a ruler dressed in highly symbolic ritual regalia.
The hieroglyphic inscription outlines the ceremonial event, when it
occurred, and the family connections of the ruler (see detail, p. 12).

Palenque, Chiapas, Mexico. Temple of the Inscriptions. The ancient Maya city of Palenque is renowned for the sophistication of its architecture and sculpture. Numerous hieroglyphic inscriptions detail the history of the site's ruling dynasty (photo by Fernando Sánchez).

served as a ground for imagery executed with mineral-pigmented slips. Motifs are generally outlined in black, filled in with orange, red, pink, gray, or purplish washes, and then fired. The covered bowl in figure 6 was manufactured during the first half of the Maya's great cultural florescence (the Classic Period), between about AD 250 and 600. The baroque imagery on the lid probably portrays the floating face of a royal ancestor—similar ancestor images are carved on stelae from the same period, where they attest to the legitimacy of a royal descendant's rule.

Court painters decorated numerous elegant ceramic vessels in the Late Classic period (about AD 600–900). Simply shaped plates, bowls, and cylindrical vessels provided the decorative field. Scenes of court life and mythological events are common subjects. Rulers are shown seated on thrones, interacting with servants, courtiers, and foreign emissaries. Ritual performances such as dances and sacrifices are also portrayed. Many of the mythological scenes have been interpreted as episodes from the Hero Twin narrative. This fascinating story was recorded in the Quiché Maya language after the Spanish Conquest but is thought to have had widespread currency in earlier times. Glyphic inscriptions were frequently painted or carved on ceramics as well. These sometimes identify the protagonists in the painted

6. Lidded Bowl with Faces of Supernaturals. Maya. About AD 250–600. Mexico or northern Central America. Earthenware with colored slips, 11″ × 14¼″ (diameter). Gift of Mr. and Mrs. Edward L. Luben; 1983.363a,b.
Maya rulers were buried with numerous offerings, including food, ritual materials (such as stingray spines and shells), and finely crafted luxury goods. Jade jewelry and high-quality ceramics were frequent funerary offerings.

7. Tripod Plate with Glyphic Text. Maya. About AD 600–900.
Mexico or northern Central America. Earthenware with colored
slips, diameter 12″. Gift of Mr. and Mrs. Morris A. Long; 1983.400.
*Maya hieroglyphic texts record dates, historical events, myth, and
astronomy. Calligraphy itself was a highly appreciated art form,
probably practiced by members of the nobility.*

scenes; often they name the vessel's function and its owner. The beautiful
calligraphy decorating the plate in figure 7 is of this character.

Clay also served as an important sculptural medium throughout Maya
history. A famous figurine tradition developed in the Campeche Coast
region of the Yucatan Peninsula. Graves excavated at burial grounds on
Jaina Island have yielded hundreds of such figurines. The finest are hand-
modeled and wear elaborate costumes and headgear. Molds were also used,
to form either heads or complete figures. The exceptionally large, mold-
made ceramic figure in figure 8 (probably from Guatemala rather than
Yucatan), has preserved much of the original pigment. Portrayed holding a
child and a monkey, this woman may represent either a noblewoman or a
female divinity.

8. Female Whistle Figure with Monkey and Child. Maya.
About AD 600–900. Guatemala. Earthenware with pigments,
13½″ × 11″ × 5½″. Funds from the Exeter Drilling Company and
Mr. and Mrs. Morris A. Long; 1979.3.
Many Maya figurines have a mouthpiece in the back and functioned
as whistles. These were probably used in festivities and ceremonies,
perhaps including funerary rites.

West Mexico

By 300 BC, the inhabitants of the West Mexican states of Colima, Nayarit, and Jalisco were also the creators of an important ceramic sculptural tradition. The West Mexicans utilized little stone in constructing their architecture, and thus even the largest sites are much eroded. From the archaeological remains, and from miniature ceramic depictions, it is known that some sites had a large circular plaza with a ceremonial platform mound in the center. On rectangular platforms around the plaza were structures with high, thatched roofs. Ceramic sculptures show that music, dance, ceremonies, and feasts took place in the plazas. Some sites also have ball courts—a version of the ancient game is still played in West Mexico today.

In and near the ceremonial plaza were dug the tombs of important families. These have a deep vertical shaft with chambers at the base. The tombs were used repeatedly over time, as significant individuals died. Placed with them were offerings of food, drink, and ornaments of shell and stone. The dead were also accompanied by ceramic sculptures in the form of plants (maguey leaves, fruits, gourds), animals (dogs, parrots, ducks, shellfish), and, most importantly, human beings. Both men and women are portrayed, often as married couples who may hold an infant or dog.

Three major stylistic groupings exist; each is named after the Mexican state in which it is most often found. Colima-style sculptures are orange or red, with smoothly modeled forms and highly polished surfaces. Jalisco figures are often enhanced with colored slips to depict costume elements and painted or tattooed body and face decorations. Jalisco figures frequently have elongated heads, disproportionately long bodies, and short limbs.

Nayarit figures incorporate several substyles. Ixtlán del Río figures generally lack the carefully smoothed forms and polished surfaces found in Colima and Jalisco. Nor are they anatomically realistic—arms and legs may be thin and ropelike, bodies are broad and chunky, and faces often have huge curved noses and toothy grimaces. Colored slips indicate body painting and patterned cloth costumes. Another substyle of Nayarit ceramics was long called Chinesco because the figures were thought to look Chinese. The figures are now called Lagunillas, after the region in Nayarit where

9. **Seated Female Figure. Nayarit, Lagunillas Style. About 200 BC–AD 300.** San Pedro Lagunillas region, Nayarit, Mexico. Earthenware with colored slips and resist decoration, 11½″ × 5¾″ × 4½″. Gift in memory of L. K. Land; 1991.488.

In West Mexico the deceased were provided with companions in clay: men, women, and children, often portrayed in festive attire or holding emblems of their social roles. Familiar domestic animals such as dogs and parrots were also placed in the tomb.

they were produced. Figure 9 shows a typically serene female figure, with a large head, broad, heavy body, and slender arms. She is simply dressed, wearing only a skirt and nose ring, but her arms, torso, and face are enhanced with painted patterns.

Another Nayarit substyle is known as Zacatecas. Zacatecas figures are seated and have short stubby legs and slender ropelike arms (figure 10).

Costumes and faces are decorated with red, tan, and black slip. After firing, figures were sometimes painted with a resist material (such as slip) in linear patterns, then held over a smoky fire. The painted patterns, protected by the slip, did not take the black coloring. When the slip was washed off, these protected areas reveal the underlying color. Male figures are distinguished by antenna-like protrusions from the head that probably represent a special coiffure.

10. Seated Couple. Zacatecas Style. About 300 BC–AD 200.
Zacatecas or Jalisco, Mexico. Earthenware with colored slips and resist decoration; 14¾″ × 7½″ × 5¼″ (female); 15″ × 8″ × 6″ (male). Florence R. and Ralph L. Burgess Trust in memory of Clayton Johns; 1990.161.1 & .2.
Zacatecas figures were often made in male-female pairs that likely represent married couples. Body painting, jewelry, and open mouths suggest singing or chanting at a social or ritual occasion. Anatomical realism was not a goal of the sculptors, as the numerous toes on both figures make clear.

Teotihuacán, Valley of Mexico. Pyramid of the Moon *(photo by Fernando Sánchez).*

Teotihuacán

Mesoamerica's greatest city arose in the Valley of Mexico, a short distance north of what is now Mexico City. At around AD 1, nearly the entire population of the valley (previously living in many scattered settlements) gathered at Teotihuacán and began a massive building program. A long, straight avenue was laid out running north-south, while another axis ran east-west. One of the very first structures built was the immense Pyramid of the Sun, still today the second largest (in volume) structure in the New World. Beneath the pyramid is a tunnel-like natural cave, which may have been interpreted as humankind's original place of emergence from the earth. Its discovery could well have inspired the population's sudden convergence at this place. In later Aztec myth, Teotihuacán was also the birthplace of the sun and moon. Other huge structures at Teotihuacán include the Pyramid of the Moon and the Ciudadela (a large plaza with a pyramid and palaces, surrounded by a platform enclosure built of stone and earth). The site also includes hundreds of smaller temple mounds and residential compounds. Teotihuacán thrived until about AD 700, when it was burned and largely abandoned.

11. Stone Serpent Heads. Teotihuacán. About AD 1–400.
Mexico. Volcanic stone. *Left:* 26½″ × 13½″ × 36″. Funds from New World Department Volunteer Fundraiser; 1971.360. *Right:* 22½″ × 13½″ × 26″. Department acquisition funds; 1962.291.
Huge stone serpents with supernatural attributes occur as architectural sculpture at Teotihuacán. The later Aztecs also decorated temples and sacred compounds with ferocious serpents. By evoking the architectural heritage of earlier cultures, the Aztecs reinforced the legitimacy of their political dominance.

Two large stone serpent heads in the Denver Art Museum's collection (figure 11) may have once ornamented a Teotihuacán pyramid, perhaps flanking a stairway. Like the carved stone supernatural serpents found at the Pyramid of Quetzalcoatl in the Ciudadela, the serpent heads are not identical to one another.

12. Mask. Teotihuacán. About AD 1–700. Mexico. Serpentine,
4⅞″ × 5⅛″. Gift of the Exeter Drilling Company; 1976.58.
The blank, enigmatic stare of Teotihuacán masks today may be
deceptive. Many probably once had inlays of shell, obsidian, or pyrite
in the eye and mouth depressions, which lent them a dramatically more
lifelike appearance.

Numerous stone masks have also been uncovered at Teotihuacán,
although lack of archaeological context means that their function is still
uncertain. Teotihuacán stone masks are idealized, with a standardized
shape and serene expression (figure 12). Their unpierced eyes and mouths
indicate that they were not worn by living individuals. Instead, they may
have been affixed to the bundled corpses of the dead in funerary ceremonies or mounted on deity images made of perishable materials.

Teotihuacán artisans produced vast quantities of ceramic goods, including vessels, figurines, and incense burners. Especially beautiful, but very
fragile, are cylindrical tripod vessels that were covered with a thin coat
of plaster after firing and brightly painted with mineral pigments in the

fresco technique. A very thin, finely made orangeware pottery was highly prized at Teotihuacán, although it seems to have been manufactured in Puebla for export to Teotihuacán. While most orangeware vessels are

13. Warrior Effigy Vessel. Teotihuacán. About AD 200–700. Mexico. Earthenware with pigment, 10¼″ × 6¼″ × 6¼″. Funds from 1986 Collectors' Choice; 1986.14a,b.

Carved stone monuments in the Maya region portray warriors in Teotihuacán garb, suggesting that the city's military might was widely known and respected. Burials of numerous sacrificed warriors have been discovered under and around the Pyramid of Quetzalcoatl in the Ciudadela at Teotihuacán.

14. Incense Burner. Teotihuacán-Maya. About AD 375–500.
Escuintla, Guatemala. Earthenware, 19″ × 14¾″ × 12″. Gift of
William I. Lee; 1985.625a,b.
This incense burner lid features a seated figure who wears elaborate
jewelry, including a necklace, earspools, and a nose ornament that
covers the lower face. Above the forehead is a butterfly with a long,
curling proboscis. Butterflies may be symbols of the human soul; many
incense burners were probably used in ancestor veneration rituals.

simply shaped, a few, like the Denver Art Museum's warrior vessel (figure 13), are complex and ornate. The pose and expression of this two-part figure, which opens at the waist, are unusually lively.

A special ceramic form was created for burning incense during religious rites. These objects have an hourglass-shaped base topped by a conical lid with a tubular, vertical chimney. The lid and chimney usually support a mold-made mask surrounded by symbolic elements (also made of clay) like butterflies, birds, hearts, and jewels. Many of these incense burners were unearthed far to the southeast of Teotihuacán, in Maya country (figure 14). Far too heavy and fragile for long-distance transportation, these Teotihuacán-style incense burners were manufactured locally, in Guatemala. The Maya were clearly in close contact with Teotihuacán (perhaps for trading purposes and/or to form political alliances). People from both cultures probably mingled in the Escuintla region in Guatemala.

THE AZTECS AND TARASCANS

The Aztec Empire ruled over much of Mesoamerica at the time of the Spanish Conquest (1519–1521). "Aztec" refers to an alliance of three central Mexican ethnic groups who occupied several towns and cities in the area that is now Mexico City. The dominant member of the Aztec Triple Alliance was the Mexica, a formerly nomadic tribal group from the north who had settled in the Valley of Mexico relatively recently. The Mexica capital, Tenochtitlán, was rebuilt after the Spanish Conquest as Mexico City. With its well-organized, powerful military, the Aztec alliance was able to subdue both neighboring and distant peoples and force them to pay tribute in the form of food, goods (including textiles and luxury items), and sacrificial victims. Rebellions against Aztec rule were common, so the Aztec state was constantly at war.

The Aztecs utilized their great wealth to build impressive architecture, including grand temple-pyramids, palaces, and schools. Large-scale stone sculpture embellished the temples and ceremonial precincts. Famous examples include the terrifying statue of Coatlicue (Serpent Skirt)—mother of the Mexica patron deity—who wears a necklace of human hands and hearts, and the huge Calendar Stone that illustrates the Aztec cosmos and creation myth.

Aztec stone sculpture is generally static in pose and compact in form, without dynamic projecting elements. Animals, including snakes, are represented frequently. Usually these animals have symbolic meanings—they represent days or months in the calendar, illustrate mythical episodes, or refer to deities. The huge fangs and tongue of the serpent in figure 15 indicate its supernatural status. In Aztec thought, snakes, which often live in holes in the ground and slither on their bellies, were closely associated with the earth.

15. Coiled Serpent. Aztec. About AD 1250–1550. Central Mexico. Volcanic stone, 10½″ × 12″ × 10¼″. Funds from Burgess Trust and various donors; 1989.8.
The rattlesnake, with its rapid strike and venomous bite, appealed to the aggressive, militaristic Aztecs.

16. *(left)* **Spouted Vessel. Tarascan. About AD 1200–1500.**
Michoacan, Mexico. Earthenware with colored slips, 9¼″ × 11″.
Department acquisition funds; 1970.310.
(right) **Tripod Rattle Bowl. Tarascan. About AD 1200–1500.**
Michoacan, Mexico. Earthenware with resist decoration, 6⅝″ × 8¼″.
Gift of Alice Tillett; 1986.158.
*The forms and decoration of Tarascan ceramics bear no resemblance to
the polychrome wares prized by the Aztecs. The Tarascans vigorously
defended their cultural, political, and economic independence in the
face of Aztec aggression.*

The Tarascan people of Michoacan successfully defended their independence from the Aztec Empire. Tzintzuntzan, the Tarascan capital, includes a series of unusual stone-faced structures, probably used for religious functions. Each of these *yatecas* consists of a rectangular platform with a circular extension projecting from one long side. Tarascan craftsmen produced bells and other objects of cast copper, and fine polychrome ceramics. Two ceramic forms are unique to the Tarascans—simple bowls supported by very large hollow legs and "teapots" with long, slender spouts and graceful arched handles (figure 16). Their smoothly burnished surfaces may be decorated with red and cream slip, and/or negative smoke-blackened designs created after firing.

The Intermediate Region

The ancient cultures of the Intermediate Region (Nicaragua, Costa Rica, Panama, Colombia) have received far less study than those of Mesoamerica to the north. While maize and beans were important foods in this region, tropical root crops such as sweet potato and manioc were also staples. Politically, the region's many peoples were organized into numerous chiefdoms, which tended to be smaller in scale and less structurally complex than states or empires. Writing was never developed or utilized in the region; thus history was not recorded until after the Spanish Conquest. Settlements in the Intermediate Region rarely achieved truly urban scale, and even public structures were built of largely perishable materials.

The artistic legacy of the region consists principally of small-scale, finely crafted luxury goods, although a few cultures developed stone sculpture traditions. Items such as decorative ceramics, ceremonial implements, and personal adornments of gold, jade, tusk, or resin were displayed, traded, and distributed as gifts. Gold in particular was exchanged over long distances—thus it is often difficult to pinpoint the origin of specific styles. Ultimately, many of these prestigious items were deposited as offerings in the graves of wealthy and powerful individuals.

Interestingly, the peoples of the Intermediate Region appear to have regarded the human body quite differently than their Mesoamerican and Andean neighbors did. In the art of those regions, human beings are almost always represented clothed or without genitals. Exposed genitals are usually a sign of humiliation, seen most often in captives. By contrast, in the Intermediate Region both males and females were often portrayed nude, with genitals displayed rather than hidden. These not only served to identify gender but also probably symbolized generative power.

Facing page: **Detail of a Conte-style plate** (figure 24).

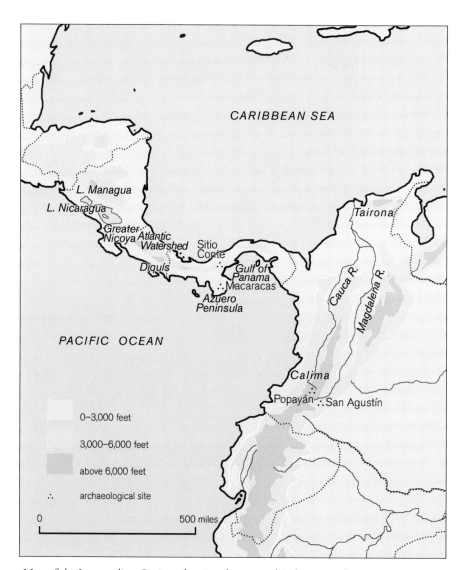

Map of the Intermediate Region, showing the geographical areas and principal archaeological sites referred to in the book.

Costa Rica

Southwest Nicaragua and northwest Costa Rica constituted a single stylistic area in ancient times (now called Greater Nicoya). By 500 BC, production of finely crafted decorative pottery had commenced in this region. Modeling, incision, slip painting, and post-fire smoke-blackening are some of the

17. Drum or Stand. Southern Greater Nicoya, Guinea Incised Style. About AD 200–500. Costa Rica. Earthenware, 11½″ × 6⅞″ (diameter). Gift of Jan and Frederick R. Mayer; 1993.529. *Variations in the firing atmosphere can create surface color irregularities, which are known as "fire-clouding." In pottery of the Guinea Incised Style, the designs were scratched into the surface after firing and emphasized with white pigment.*

techniques employed in the region's many pottery styles. Figure 17 is simply shaped and may have served as a pot stand or drum. After the vessel was formed, it was allowed to dry until leather-hard, then carefully burnished. After firing, linear decorations were scratched into the surface. The effect is elegant, but the meaning of the incised design is unknown.

Figure 18, from the Atlantic Watershed region (eastern Costa Rica), portrays a nude male figure holding a severed head. Bold body painting or

18. Warrior Figure with Trophy Head. Atlantic Watershed, La Selva Style. About AD 500–1000. Costa Rica. Resist-decorated earthenware, 14⅞″ × 7⅜″ × 7¼″. Lent by Jan and Frederick R. Mayer; 246.1992.

Proud and aggressive, with huge feet firmly planted, the warrior displays a human head. Its small size suggests that the head may be shrunken, although this practice is not ethnographically documented in Central America. Human head effigies were also made of stone and ceramic.

tattooing covers much of the stocky body, as well as the face. The severed head he displays is likely that of an enemy killed in battle. Conceivably, however, the head may be the cherished relic of a revered ancestor. Such a relic might have conferred protection and spiritual power on descendants.

19. **Tubular Bead. Atlantic Watershed. About** AD 300–700.
Costa Rica. Jadeitic albitite, 12⅛″ × 1¼″ × 1⅝″. Gift of Jan and
Frederick R. Mayer; 1994.654.
Hard green stones were prized by both Costa Ricans and their
Mesoamerican neighbors to the north. Although Olmec and Maya
jades have been discovered in Costa Rica, they are sometimes reworked,
or even sawed into much smaller pieces.

Numerous jade ornaments have been discovered in high-status Costa
Rican tombs. Some are clearly Olmec or early Classic Maya in style and
must have been treasured imports. Most Costa Rican jades appear to
have been manufactured locally, although the geological source of the raw
material is still uncertain. (A major source of jadeite was recently discovered in Guatemala.) Many Costa Rican jade ornaments were originally
worked into a celt (axe blade) form. Subsequently, the celt was sawed
lengthwise into two or more pieces that were decoratively carved and
drilled for suspension as pendants. Pendants of humans, deities, and birds
and other animals are common. Less intricate, but perhaps even more
impressive, are large, tubular jade beads, probably worn horizontally across
the chest. Raised bands encircling the tubes resemble bindings of leather or
cloth. The bead in figure 19 is decorated with two grimacing, opposed,
crouching figures. Made of a very tough material and sometimes over a
foot in length, these beads are drilled longitudinally. Accomplished using
only a drill and grit, this was an arduous, lengthy task. Ownership of such
an ornament must have conveyed considerable prestige.

Production of jade ornaments in Costa Rica largely ceased around
AD 700. About the same time, goldworking technology was introduced

20. **Bell Pendant. Diquís. About** AD **700–1550.** Costa Rica. Gold,
diameter 2⅞″. Gift of Jan and Frederick R. Mayer; 1996.109.
This bell takes the form of a powerful supernatural creature, with a
jaguar head, a round body that forms the bell chamber, and a
triangular bird's tail. Four smaller heads radiating from the body are
positioned like limbs. Strange profile creatures with long, curved tails
and bird beaks encircle the central figure.

to Central America from South America. Artisans used both gold and
gold-copper alloy to produce showy ornaments. Hammered into sheets,
then cut, punched, and embossed, gold was formed into disks, collars, and
diadems. Pendants, sometimes very large and heavy, were created by the
lost wax process. The artist first modeled the desired form in wax, then
encased it in clay to form a mold. When heated, the wax melted out, leaving a cavity into which the molten metal was poured. After cooling, the
mold was broken away, and the gold ornament was polished. Since each
mold was used only once, every cast ornament is unique. Artists of the
Diquís region of southwest Costa Rica took full advantage of wax's mal-
leability and ornamented their forms with balls, rolls, strips, and braids of

21. **Catfish Pendant. Diquís. About AD 700–1550.** Costa Rica. Gold,
4¼″ × 2¹⁄₁₆″ × ½″. Gift of Jan and Frederick R. Mayer; 1995.718.
*Barbels beside the mouth suggest a catfish identification for this
pendant. Serpents with serrated bodies emerge from the mouth,
however, suggesting special powers.*

wax to create intricate openwork compositions (figure 20). The human
beings and animals depicted in Diquís goldwork are rarely naturalistic.
Instead, traits of various creatures are often combined, and powerful ema-
nations radiate from mouths, limbs, belts, and genitals (figure 21).

Eastern Costa Rica, known as the Atlantic Watershed region, was a major
center for the production of stone sculpture. The available stone in this
area is volcanic, with a coarse, porous texture. It is thus unsuitable for finely

22. Metate in Form of Jaguar. Atlantic Watershed. About AD
300–700. Costa Rica. Stone, 11⅝" × 17¾" × 37½". Gift of Jan and
Frederick R. Mayer; 1995.582.
*Felines, especially jaguars, were revered as powerful, stealthy hunters
throughout the pre-Columbian world. Kings and chiefs wore jaguar
pelts proudly, as symbols of their own nobility and fierceness. Seated
atop a jaguar metate, a Costa Rican ruler asserted his dominance over
both men and nature.*

detailed relief carving like that for which the Maya are famous. Instead,
most sculpture is three-dimensional, sometimes embellished with simple
raised patterns. Stocky human figures, generally nude or scantily dressed, are
presented in a variety of poses. Male figures are often depicted as warriors,
holding trophy heads and weapons, or as prisoners with bound hands.
Head effigies may have served as permanent reminders of victory in battle.
Female figures often hold their breasts, probably in reference to fertility.

Among the most impressive works of sculpture from this region are
metates, or grinding stones, which were carved from a single block of
stone. Some are carved in the form of a feline (figure 22), bird, peccary, or
other animal, with the animal's back serving as the grinding surface. The
most elaborate examples, called flying-panel metates, have openwork birds,
animals, and human figures below the grinding surface. The large, highly
decorated metates may well have served as high-status seats, emphasizing
the leaders' role as providers and controllers of sustenance.

Panama's prehispanic archaeological heritage has been less extensively studied that that of Mesoamerica or the Andes. Lacking any tradition of monumental architecture or sculpture, Panama is best known for polychrome ceramics and ornaments of cast or hammered gold. Sitio Conte, an archaeological site in central Panama, was explored in the first half of the century by teams from Harvard and the University of Pennsylvania. Spectacularly rich graves were unearthed there that yielded much information on social structure, burial practices, and artistic production. Society was stratified: the most powerful individuals were interred with numerous human attendants and lavish offerings of polychrome pottery and gold ornaments, including helmets, breastplates, wristguards, pendants, and beaded necklaces. Other valuable materials placed in the Sitio Conte graves include

23. Breastplate. Conte Style. About AD 450–900. Parita, Azuero Peninsula, Panama. Gold, diameter 5¼″. Department acquisition funds; 1965.196.
The grimacing creature on this breastplate has long been known as the Crocodile God. Recent research suggests that the figure may represent an iguana with supernatural attributes.

turtle carapaces, stingray spines, whale teeth, shark teeth, boar tusks, bone, agate, quartz, emerald, and serpentine.

Hammered gold breastplates from Sitio Conte, usually round or square in shape, are decorated with intricate embossed images of part-human, part-animal beings with claws, bared teeth, and serpentine, serrated appendages (figure 23). Closely similar beings, often in dynamic poses, are painted on polychrome pottery from the same region. Common shapes include jars, plates, and pedestal bowls. Modeled effigy vessels portraying humans or birds, crustaceans, and other animals are less frequent but are painted in the same palette of black, red, and purple on a cream-slipped ground. The imagery on the plate in figure 24 is unusual—human footprints in circular paths.

24. Plate with Footprint Motif. Conte Style. About AD 500–1000.
Central Panama. Earthenware with colored slips, 2⅜″ × 13⅝″
(diameter). Gift of Mr. and Mrs. I. J. Shore; 1991.1270.
The circular paths on this plate suggest the movements of dancers in a plaza, or perhaps a ritual procession. Curiously, however, only the prints of left feet are represented (see detail, p. 38).

San Agustín, Colombia. *Alto de las Piedras stone sculptures. Both portray male figures, one (left) with crossed fangs, the other with a strange, two-headed creature clinging to his head and back (photos courtesy of Dr. Armand Labbé).*

COLOMBIA

Colombia's most famous archaeological zone is San Agustín, located in the Magdalena River valley of western Colombia. The sites in this region include earthen mounds and monumental tombs, their chambers lined and roofed with large stone slabs. Inside some of these tomb chambers were great stone statues, both male and female, many grasping weapons or ceremonial implements. Some wear masks, while others, with prominent crossed fangs, probably represent supernatural beings. Fierce animals rise from the backs of some figures; possibly they represent protective spirits or alter egos.

Several of San Agustín's stone figures wear necklaces, ear ornaments, or nose ornaments, or carry gourd-shaped lime containers (coca leaf, chewed

25. Feline Effigy Vessel. Calima, Ilama Style. About 1000 BC–AD 1.
Upper Cauca River valley, Colombia. Burnished and incised
earthenware, 8½″ × 5⅞″ × 8¾″. Bequest of Robert J. Stroessner;
1992.59.
The incised patterns on the feline's body (typical of the Ilama Style) are
reminiscent of textiles or basketry. Because of Colombia's humid climate,
however, very few artifacts made of organic materials have survived.

with mineral lime, enhances the body's ability to withstand pain and
fatigue). Jewelry and containers were often made of cast or hammered gold,
as evidenced by the large quantities of ancient Colombian goldwork in
museum collections. Most of the gold was collected from streambeds, then

alloyed with copper to produce a tougher, more easily worked material. A pure gold surface was produced on finished ornaments by soaking them in a bath of acidic plant juices. This process leached away copper molecules in the surface layer, leaving behind the more stable gold. Different colored gold alloys were also used for decorative effect in certain cast-gold objects. Manufacturing techniques utilized by the ancient artisans included hammering, annealing, repoussé, chasing, soldering, and lost wax casting.

Over a span of at least fifteen hundred years, an array of visually spectacular styles was developed in Colombia. Calima goldworkers from west-central Colombia (about AD 1–800) specialized in ornaments of sheet gold with complex shapes, repoussé faces and decorative patterns, and dangling attached elements. Headdresses, pectorals, and tweezers must have shimmered magnificently in the sunlight. Masterful Quimbaya artisans (about AD 500–1000) used gold-copper alloy to cast large lime containers (up to twelve inches tall). Some take the form of sublimely beautiful human figures with smooth, nude bodies and serene expressions. The Tairona style of northern Colombia (about AD 900–1550) is best known for cast-gold ear and nose ornaments with intricate openwork spirals and braids, and for pendants that portray masked human figures with dramatic openwork headgear.

Ancient Colombian ceramics have been long overshadowed by the region's abundant goldwork, but these inventive and sophisticated ceramic traditions are finally receiving increased recognition and study. The most characteristic and recognizable Calima form (the *alcarraza*) is a small jar with short diverging spouts separated by an arched handle. The body of the jar may be simple and round, or modeled in the form of humans, animals, or fruits, with incised and/or painted decoration. The feline alcarraza in figure 25 is covered with delicate crosshatched and stippled patterns that may represent a jaguar's pelt.

One of the most impressive known examples of Colombian ceramic art is a seated male figure from the Popayán region of west-central Colombia (figure 26). Stools were important symbols of rank in both the Intermediate Region and the Caribbean. The figure's commanding pose, elaborate headdress and shield, and gold necklace together suggest an individual of wealth

and power. His swollen calves reflect the use of ligatures (bands) tied below the knee and at the ankle. Amazonian peoples today use ligatures to strengthen muscles. The crested, lizardlike creature clinging to the figure's back recalls the animals that often rise behind San Agustín stone figures.

Above and facing page: **26. Figure Seated on a Bench. Popayán. Before AD 1500.** Cauca River valley, Colombia. Earthenware with slip, 15″ × 9″ × 12½″. Gift of Mr. and Mrs. Edward M. Strauss in memory of Alan Lapiner; 1977.62.

The huge hands and feet and exaggerated, swollen calves of this figure (probably a chief) suggest solidity, strength, and capacity for action.

Andean South America

Complex societies, urban populations, and sophisticated artistic traditions also developed in the central Andean region of western South America, despite the many challenges posed by the natural environment. The Andean mountain range separates a narrow coastal strip along the Pacific from the vast Amazon basin. Moist, warm air from the Amazon is blocked by the mountains, and the cool air over the Pacific (affected by the cold Humboldt Current) drops little rain on the coast. As a consequence, the coast is a desert, with human occupation concentrated in the valleys of rivers that descend from the mountains. Irrigation with these waters permits agriculture, while the cold ocean waters off the coast nourish abundant marine life. Life in the highlands is dramatically affected by altitude. At the highest elevations, agriculture is impossible, but pastures support large herds of domesticated camelids—llamas and alpacas. At lower elevations a wide range of crops were cultivated, including potatoes, quinoa, and even maize. Coca, an important ritual and medicinal crop, was often grown on the warm eastern slopes of the Andes. The peoples of the Andean coast, highlands, and eastern lowlands maintained regular contact with one another through trade and kinship ties, which facilitated the exchange of products from the varied ecological zones. Alpaca fiber produced in the highlands and cotton grown on the coast supplied the materials for one of the world's greatest textile traditions. Religious ideas, technologies, and finished goods also circulated, their dissemination sometimes occurring in conjunction with political alliance or military conquest.

Ancestor veneration accompanied by elaborate mortuary practices was pervasive in the ancient Andes. Corpses were carefully prepared and provided with lavish offerings of food, clothing, and other goods. The

---

Facing page: **Detail of a Wari tunic** (figure 36).

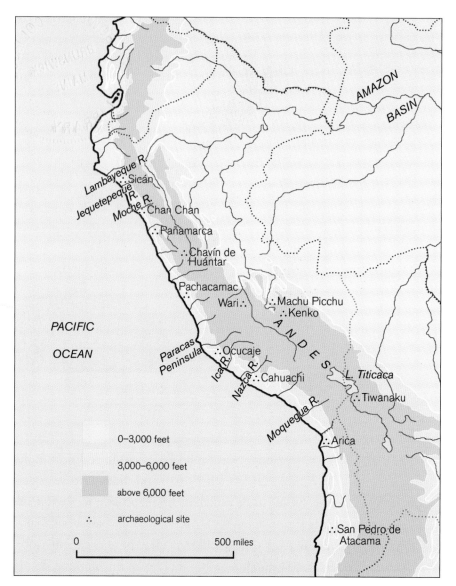

Map of Andean South America, showing the geographical areas and principal archaeological sites referred to in the book.

extremely dry burial conditions on much of the coast account for the extraordinary preservation of many organic materials, including wood, basketry, cloth, and even feathers. Most of the beautifully crafted objects in museum collections were preserved in tombs.

Chavín de Huántar, Peru. Temple (photo by Fernando Sánchez).

CHAVÍN AND PERU'S NORTH COAST

For many years, various ceramic styles found at archaeological sites in the valleys of Peru's north coast were labeled Chavín and thought to be associated with the culture of Chavín de Huántar (900–200 BC), located in the northern highlands. It is now known that much of the coastal material is actually earlier than Chavín itself. Tembladera-style pottery (about 1500–900 BC) from the Jequetepeque Valley is usually gray in color and decorated with modeling, incising, and sometimes resinous paints applied after firing. Bottles are the most highly decorated form and have either a tall, slender neck or a stirrup-shaped spout (figure 27). For more than two millennia, stirrup-spout bottles remained the pre-eminent form for north coast prestige ceramics.

The Chavín civilization represents the culmination of centuries of cultural and artistic development in north and central Peru. Located high in

27. Stirrup-Spout Bottle. Tembladera Style. About 1500–900 BC.
Jequetepeque Valley, Peru. Earthenware, 9¾" × 6" (diameter).
Bequest of Robert J. Stroessner; 1992.91.
This hand-modeled vessel is complex in form: the doughnut-shaped
chamber has lobed protrusions that bear incised faces. The grimacing
heads at the base of the spout were decorated with resin-based pigments.

the Andes, the site of Chavín de Huántar controlled an important route
linking the eastern lowlands with the highlands and the coast. The presence of a massive stone temple and numerous carved stone monuments
representing deities and supernatural beings indicates that Chavín was a
major religious center. Chavín's earliest cult image, known as the Lanzón,
is a bladelike shaft of granite more than thirteen feet tall. The deity carved
on the Lanzón has a grinning mouth with huge fangs, hair in the form of
snakes, and clawed hands and feet. Located inside a narrow passage deep
within the temple, it probably served as a powerful oracle. Pilgrims from

distant regions traveled to Chavín to consult the oracle and participate in religious rituals. Felines, snakes, and caimans (all dangerous predatory animals) appear frequently in Chavín religious art in stone, gold, and textiles, and they clearly conveyed spiritual potency.

THE PARACAS AND NASCA CIVILIZATIONS

Chavín's religious ideas, and the art through which they were expressed, were highly influential. Textiles painted with Chavín imagery have been discovered hundreds of miles away on Peru's south coast. Fanged felines, snakes, and other symbols present in Chavín art also occur in textiles and ceramics of the Paracas civilization (about 200 BC–AD 200) of the south coast.

The Paracas people built no large-scale public architecture and are best known for spectacular embroidered garments interred with the dead. The corpse was buried in seated position, wrapped in layers of cloth, leaves, and embroidered garments. The mummy bundles of some individuals (presumably the wealthiest, most important members of society) contained dozens of richly embroidered garments and hundreds of yards of undecorated cloth.

Two major styles of embroidery exist: linear and block color. In linear-style textiles, nested images such as birds, felines, and serpents are created with parallel lines of stitching in red, gold, green, and blue. In block color embroideries, the subject matter is broader, including birds, fish, mammals, and humans or supernaturals wearing elaborate costumes and accouterments. Embroidered on the mantle in figure 28 are flying supernatural beings, with bird wings and tails, that grasp severed human heads. Sacrifice by decapitation was practiced by many Andean cultures. The deified forces of nature were nourished and assuaged by the offering of human life, and heads were likened to seeds or fruit. The multicolored block color images are composed of outlined shapes filled in with closely spaced stitches. The brightly dyed yarns used in Paracas garments are probably alpaca. These animals are raised in the highlands, not on the coast near Paracas. In all likelihood, the Paracas people exchanged coastal products desired by highlanders for the alpaca yarns they needed.

28. Mantle. Paracas. About 100 BC–AD 200. South coast, Peru. Cotton fabric, camelid fiber embroidery (probably alpaca), 48⅝″ × 88″. Funds from Alvin and Geraldine Cohen, Tom and Noël Congdon, Mr. and Mrs. Samuel Gary, Hannah Levy, Mr. and Mrs. Morris A. Long, Jan and Frederick R. Mayer, Myron and Louann Miller, Neusteter Institute Fund, Margaret Powers, Mrs. Charles Rosenbaum, Mr. and Mrs. Irving Shwayder, Mr. and Mrs. Edward M. Strauss, Mr. and Mrs. Thomas Taplin, and the Volunteer Endowment Fund; 1980.44.

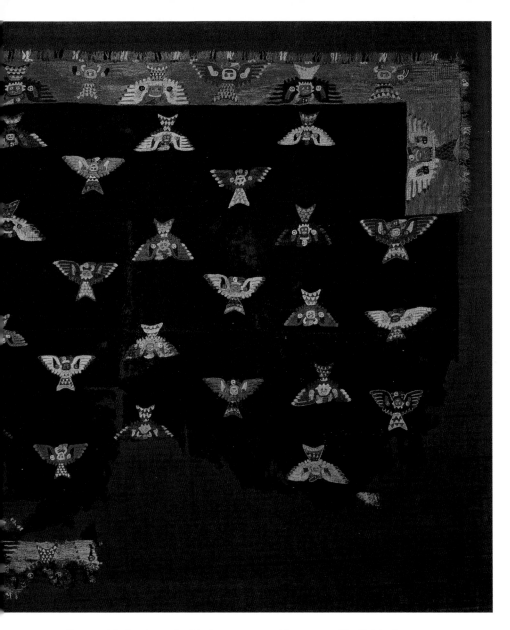

Paracas block color embroideries were created by groups of individuals. A master designer selected the design layout and color combinations (which were often extremely complex). After the motif outlines were stitched by expert embroiderers, the colors could be filled in by less experienced hands.

29. Incised Jar. Paracas, Ocucaje Style. About 200 BC–AD 200.
South coast, Peru. Earthenware with pigments, 13″ × 12″ (diameter).
Gift of Jan and Frederick R. Mayer; 1970.237.
*This large vessel is well potted, with thin, strong walls. Close inspection
reveals the diagonal strokes used to smooth the exterior.*

Paracas decorative pottery forms include bowls, jars, and bottles with two
small spouts joined by a slender strap handle. The bottle's chamber may
be simple and round, or modeled in the shape of a gourd, bird, or feline.
Surfaces may be smoothly burnished, or incised with linear patterns and
colored resinous paints applied after firing. The jar in figure 29, from the
Ocucaje region of the Ica River valley, is boldly incised with large birds.
After firing, dots of resist material were applied to the birds' outlines and
bodies. Finally, the vessel was smoked over a fire, and the resist material was
removed to reveal the underlying clay color.

30. **Human Figure Drum. Proto-Nasca. About 100 BC–AD 200.**
South coast, Peru. Earthenware, 16¾" × 9¼" (diameter). Funds
from the Marion Hendrie estate; 1972.189.
Music was an important component of Nasca ritual. Numerous pan-
pipes have been discovered at Cahuachi, an early Nasca pilgrimage site.

The Nasca people (about AD 1–700), who inhabited coastal valleys south
of Paracas, can be regarded as the cultural successors of the Paracas people.
They are best known for the Nasca Lines, large-scale geoglyphs traced on
the barren plateau above the inhabited Nazca River valley. Most are straight
lines, but living forms were also depicted, including monkeys, whales, and
spiders. An astronomical significance is possible.

Early Nasca decorative ceramics have incised design outlines filled in with
colored slips applied before firing. The colors are limited: black, brown,
tan, and cream. Effigy bottles, which portray birds and other animals,

31. Female Effigy Vessel. Nasca. About AD 300–600. South coast, Peru. Earthenware with colored slips, 5½″ × 4½″ (diameter). Gift of Mr. and Mrs. Frank S. Simons; 1969.289.
Late Nasca potters created bottles portraying men and women with attributes of wealth (such as fine textiles) and power (such as trophy heads). This likely reflects increased stratification within Nasca society.

fruits, and costumed humans, usually have a single spout and a strap handle. Figure 30 shows a very rare form: a ceramic drum. An animal skin was stretched over the large mouth of the vessel, which would have been played in an inverted position. The drum's simply modeled chamber portrays a masked ceremonialist wearing a headcloth with embroidered borders and carrying a small baton and a wand with dangling elements.

Later Nasca decorated pottery has painted rather than incised outlines and a much wider range of slip colors. Bowls, jars, and double spout-and-bridge bottles are common, as are modeled effigies of humans and animals. The bottle in figure 31 portrays a woman wearing decorative garments and holding a mirror (probably of polished pyrite, an iron ore, or anthracite, a form of coal). Painted subject matter is diverse, and includes animals, supernaturals, and humans involved in agriculture, fishing, warfare, and other activities. Nasca weavers were virtuosos who produced garments using a variety of extraordinarily complex techniques. Designs range from large-scale geometric patterns to elaborately costumed human and supernatural figures.

The Moche and Recuay Civilizations

On Peru's north coast, the Moche people were the approximate contemporaries (about AD 1–700) of the Paracas and Nasca. Seemingly, the region was not politically unified, but rather divided into several competitive local kingdoms. Public architecture was constructed with adobe bricks; the largest examples are the huge Pyramids of the Sun and Moon in the Moche River valley. These probably served ritual, administrative, and elite residential functions. Colorful murals painted with mineral pigments on plastered adobe walls are preserved at a few Moche sites. A famous scene from Pañamarca depicts a sacrificial ritual (known as the Presentation Theme) that involves both human and mythological characters. Costume elements and implements discovered in elite tombs at several Moche sites suggest that the buried individuals may have performed roles in similar rituals.

Moche society was hierarchical, and members of the elite were buried with lavish quantities of finely crafted luxury goods produced by specialist artisans. Gold and silver were fashioned into exquisite necklaces and ornaments for the ears and nose. Large adornments for headdresses, shields, and the small of the back were often made of gold-copper alloy. Depletion gilding made them shine like pure gold. Moche decorative ceramics were also common burial offerings. Stirrup-spout bottles were a common form and were frequently manufactured with the use of press molds. Some vessel chambers are highly sculptural. Birds, mammals, fish, crustaceans, and human beings are all portrayed, as well as complex multifigural scenes in architectural or natural settings. Portrait vessels with highly individualized features usually depict males (probably rulers), but females were also portrayed occasionally. Some of these vessels are true portraits, which depict

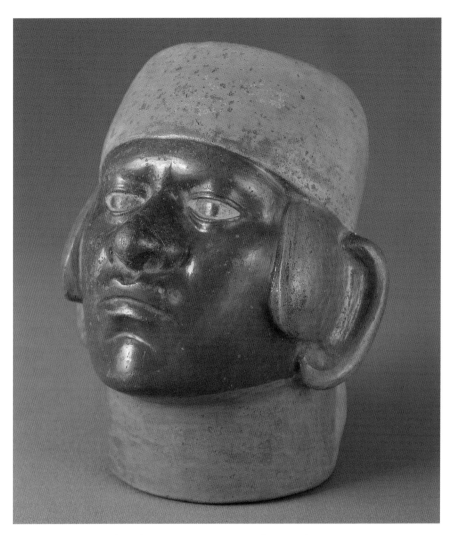

32. Portrait Jar. Moche. About AD 300–600. North coast, Peru.
Earthenware with colored slips, 7″ × 4¾″ (diameter). Gift of Mr.
and Mrs. Morris A. Long; 1985.410.
*Several portraits of this individual (who has distinctive scars on his upper
lip) are known. He is portrayed as a child and as an adult, wearing high-
status costume elements like ear ornaments and patterned headcloths.
Here, these adornments have been removed, probably prior to sacrifice.*

recognizable individuals (sometimes at more than one stage of life). Moche
expert Christopher Donnan has suggested that the simple headdress, and
ears with ornaments removed, may indicate that the individual in figure 32

has been captured and prepared for sacrificial execution. Simply shaped vessels were often decorated with dynamic painted scenes, usually in red or brown on a cream-slipped background. Depictions of warfare, hunting, religious ceremonies, and mythological events provide a glimpse of elite activities and beliefs.

The Recuay culture (about AD 1–650) developed in the upper reaches of Peru's north coast river valleys and the adjacent highlands. Large-scale Recuay sculpture consists of carved lintels and stone slabs with low-relief depictions of warriors and felines. Luxury goods deposited in wealthy Recuay tombs include carved stone bowls and fine jewelry. But, like the Moche, the Recuay are best known for their decorative pottery. Usually manufactured with fine white clay, Recuay vessels were painted with red, orange, and black slip. Additional patterns were created after firing by painting with a resist material, then smoking over a fire. Like Moche ceramics, fancy Recuay vessels were often modeled in the form of animals or people, or as multifigural scenes. Recuay modeling is generally more folklike than that of the Moche, however. The bottle in figure 33 depicts an event centered on a male figure whose importance is signaled by his frontal pose, scepter, patterned tunic, elaborate headgear, and jewelry. He is flanked on either side by cupbearing female attendants. A fourth male figure also serves as the vessel's spout. The geometric painted patterns below the figures probably represent the decorated walls of the structure in which the scene occurs.

Recuay stone lintel. Museo Arqueológico de Ancash (photo by Fernando Sánchez).

33. Vessel with Human Figures. Recuay. About AD 1–650.
Northern highlands, Peru. Earthenware with colored slips and resist
decoration, 8¼″ × 7″ (diameter). Gift of Rose Kushei; 1961.87.
The female figures on this vessel offer cups to a scepter-bearing male.
The bottle itself may have been used for pouring an intoxicating
beverage like corn beer, which was essential to Andean social, ritual,
and political gatherings.

Tiwanaku, Bolivia. *Gateway of the Sun, detail (photo by Fernando Sánchez).*

TIWANAKU AND WARI

In the south-central highlands, in what is now Bolivia, arose one of the most influential Andean civilizations. Tiwanaku (AD 200–1000), located near Lake Titicaca, is distinguished by large stone-faced mounds and courts, impressive monolithic portals, and columnar stone statues. Tiwanaku's most famous monument, the Gateway of the Sun, is decorated with a complex relief-carved composition. At the center, in high relief, is Tiwanaku's rayed-face principal deity standing atop a stepped pyramid. Arrays of low-relief attendants in running or kneeling poses flank the deity. They too are supernatural: winged humans, and birds carrying staffs. Tiwanaku's stone figures, which likely portray rulers or their ancestors, are rendered wearing patterned tapestry garments. In their hands they sometimes hold ceremonial drinking cups, or trays used for mixing hallucinogenic snuffs.

Tiwanaku, Bolivia. Ponce Monolith
(photo by Fernando Sánchez).

Hallucinogenic snuff provided a means of access to the supernatural world of ancestors and nature spirits. The snuff tray in figure 34 is extraordinarily lavish, with a three-dimensional supernatural animal (that once grasped a severed human head) on the handle. Incised designs, gold sheathing, and inlays of stone, shell, and gold enhance both the animal and the rim of the oval mixing tray. The frequency of decapitation imagery in Tiwanaku snuff-taking equipment and tapestry tunics indicates the importance of human sacrifice in Tiwanaku religious ritual.

Tiwanaku-style artifacts, including textiles, baskets, and carved wooden cups and snuff trays, have been discovered at sites on the arid western Andean slopes and coast of southern Peru and northern Chile. From these warmer regions, Tiwanaku obtained crops like maize and probably other materials unavailable in the Titicaca Basin. Some of these Tiwanaku-influenced sites were probably colonies, while others may have been merely trading partners.

Northwest of Tiwanaku in Peru's central highlands is the site of Wari, capital of a politically and culturally influential state (about AD 650–800).

Wari architecture is very different from that of Tiwanaku, with narrow, almost mazelike passageways and very tall stone walls. Wari's people probably adopted a version of Tiwanaku's religion, along with the system of religious symbols used to communicate those beliefs. Stylistically, however, Wari art can be distinguished from that of Tiwanaku. Wari ceramics are very well crafted, with bright, multicolored slips and sharply delineated images. Figure 35 shows a bottle in the form of a spondylus shell (a sacred and valuable material used for offerings) painted with the rayed face of the principal Tiwanaku/Wari deity.

Wari weavers, probably working in state-sponsored workshops, produced very fine, vividly colored tapestry tunics (figure 36). These were generally woven with warps of cotton and wefts of alpaca fiber. Alpaca fiber takes dye readily; vibrant reds, pinks, and yellows were especially favored. The imagery on Wari tunics is often derived from that seen on Tiwanaku's Gateway of the Sun. Wari weavers deliberately altered these images, however, to create abstract, visually striking designs whose subject matter can be difficult to recognize.

34. Snuff Tray. Early Tiwanaku. About AD 200–400. Northern Chile. Wood, stone, shell, gold, 2¾″ × 3³⁄₁₆″ × 6¾″. Department acquisition funds; 2000.211.
Analysis of residues on Tiwanaku-style snuff trays has revealed the presence of chemicals contained in anadenanthera tree seeds. When inhaled through the nostrils, the snuff produces visions.

Wari artifacts (and local imitations) have been discovered at sites far from the capital. This is often cited as evidence that the Wari state was a militaristic empire (much like that of the later Inca) that imposed a new religion and art style on conquered peoples. Alternatively, the wide distribution of Wari-style goods may indicate cultural and religious prestige and the existence of a highly developed trade network.

35. Shell-Form Canteen with Deity Face. Wari. About AD 650–800. Peru. Earthenware with colored slips, 7¼" × 5¼" × 3½". Gift of Olive Bigelow by exchange; 1996.35.
The spondylus mollusk lives in warm ocean waters, so it is not found off the coast of Peru. Instead, these "spiny oysters" were imported into Peru from what is now Ecuador. The shells were prized for their bright orange color.

36. Tunic. Wari. About AD 650–800. Peru. Interlocked tapestry with cotton warps, camelid fiber wefts, 81½″ × 40½″. Funds from 1986 Collectors' Choice; 1986.15.
Woven with very fine, densely packed threads, Wari tapestry tunics were extremely labor-intensive. Several weavers worked side by side to produce a wide panel of cloth. Two panels were stitched together to create a tunic (see detail, p. 54).

SICÁN

After the decline of Moche civilization on Peru's north coast, several important states arose in the region. The Sicán polity (about AD 800–1350) was centered in the Lambayeque Valley, where numerous large adobe pyramid

37. **Large Cups. Sicán or Chimú. About** AD 800–1550. North
coast, Peru. Silver. *Left:* 7″ × 7½″(diameter). Gift of Jan and
Frederick R. Mayer; 1969.303. *Right:* 6″ × 5½″ (diameter).
Department acquisition funds; 1969.302.
*Iconographically, these two silver cups are the most complex extant
artworks from ancient Peru's north coast. Dense imagery involving
both humans and supernaturals covers not only the vessels' walls, but
also the bottoms.*

mounds were built. Urban populations were supported by a highly productive agricultural sector, made possible in turn by an extensive, technically
sophisticated irrigation system. Mold-made pottery (generally blackware or
painted with red designs on a cream-slipped ground) was produced in
large-scale workshops. Textiles were probably also manufactured in state-
controlled workshops. Tapestry from this region has cotton warps, and wefts
of both cotton and camelid fiber. Complex scenes rendered in this technique depict activities such as spinning and weaving, warfare, seafaring,
and religious or civic rituals.

Sicán artisans also practiced metallurgy on a large scale. Copper, bronze,
silver, and gold were fashioned into a variety of implements and ornaments. Most famous are knives with semicircular blades, and handles in the
form of a lavishly dressed figure with comma-shaped eyes. Dubbed the
"Lord of Sicán," this being is thought to be the principal Sicán deity. Two
heavily decorated silver cups (figure 37) were created by metalworkers from

Sicán, or perhaps from the slightly later Chimú Kingdom (about AD 1100–1550). Both are formed of sheet silver with repoussé decoration created by pushing out from the inside surface of the metal. The imagery on each vessel is extremely complex. One cup features roundels with scenes involving spondylus shell. Below them may be a procession with litters, a cupbearer, and a figure displaying crops. Imagery on the other cup is even more complex: a giant serpent filled with fish may represent a river. Architectural compounds, gardens, boats, deer hunters, and supernatural beings are all included in what may be the episodes of a mythological story.

Machu Picchu, Peru. Temple (photo by Fernando Sánchez).

THE INCA

The Inca ascent to power in the century before the Spanish Conquest in the 1530s is astonishing. A small ethnic group from the southern highlands of Peru, the Inca managed to conquer first their immediate neighbors, and eventually a vast territory extending from Ecuador in the north to Chile in

38. Large Jug. Inca. About AD 1400–1532. Peru. Earthenware with
colored slips, 30″ × 21½″ (diameter). Funds from the Burgess Trust,
Walt Disney Imagineering, Alianza de las Artes Americanas, and
Jan and Frederick R. Mayer; 1993.25.
*The painted decoration on this exceptionally large vessel is unusually
ornate and includes both flamingos and insects. The lug at the base of
the neck is modeled in the form of a feline head (see detail, p. 6).*

39. Ear Ornaments. Chimú-Inca. About AD 1450–1532. North coast, Peru. Gold; 3⁵⁄₁₆″ × 1⅞″ (diameter); 3¼″ × 1¹³⁄₁₆″ (diameter). Gift of Mr. and Mrs. Edward M. Strauss in honor of Robert Stroessner; 1991.1018a,b.

Within the multiethnic Inca empire, dress was strictly regulated and reflected both ethnicity and rank. Only nobles were permitted to wear ear ornaments. The Spanish called these nobles orejones *(big ears) because of their stretched earlobes.*

the south. The numerous ethnic groups and independent political entities were not only conquered, but effectively integrated into a centrally administered political and economic system. This achievement was unmatched anywhere in the Americas until Spain's conquest and colonization of an even larger territory.

Today, the Inca are best known for their architecture, with its massive blocks of precisely cut and fitted stone. Inca reverence for the landscape (which they perceived to be animated by spiritual forces often ancestral to human groups) is evident at sites like Kenko and Machu Picchu, where natural rock outcrops are enshrined by manmade stonework.

Inca-style goods carried great prestige throughout the empire. High-quality textiles (especially tapestry) were distributed to loyal vassals and imperial administrators. Distinctively shaped and painted Inca ceramics were visible symbols of cultural and political affiliation. The *arybalo* is an emblematic Inca vessel form made in both large (figure 38) and small sizes. Used for storing and serving liquids, including corn beer, arybalos functioned within a system of ritualized reciprocal obligations. At every level of government, leaders were expected to provide feasts for their subordinates, who in turn owed labor, military service, and allegiance. Corn beer was the most essential component of such feasts; serving it from a large and elaborately decorated arybalo emphasized the wealth and generosity of the Inca state.

Peoples conquered by the Inca and incorporated into their empire often retained many elements of their indigenous culture and identity. The wealthy Chimú Kingdom of the north coast, for example, continued to be an important center for manufacturing and exporting under Inca domination. A pair of gold ear ornaments (figure 39) was probably made by north coast craftsmen in this period. The long shafts are decorated with birds and waves, while the round fronts feature male figures wearing short, wide tunics and large headdresses. The figures wear masks that dangle from hinges, suggesting that the figures are shown participating in a ritual.

The Spanish Conquest

Spain's conquest of the New World commenced with the Caribbean and continued in Mexico, Central America, and South America. The toppling of the mighty but fragile Aztec Empire occurred in 1521; the Inca Empire, weakened by civil war and smallpox (which arrived in advance of the Spanish invaders), collapsed in 1536. Several decades more were required to defeat pockets of military resistance. Spanish imposition of new political and economic systems, and Christianity, required far longer. Although Europeans dominated governmental and church hierarchies and controlled much of the conquered territories' productive resources, the indigenous peoples retained some social and political power and managed to preserve many elements of their culture. The indigenous nobility's privileges and rights to land and labor were often respected by Spanish authority. Technologies, domesticated plants and animals, and religious beliefs introduced by the Spanish did not simply replace their native counterparts. Instead, European, indigenous, and sometimes African cultures were gradually integrated to create new societies. These were different from that of Spain, and different from one another as well. This rich cultural intermingling is evident in the diverse nations of Latin America today.

Further Reading

Alva, Walter and Christopher Donnan
1993 *Royal Tombs of Sipan.* Los Angeles: Fowler Museum of Cultural History, University of California.

Benson, Elizabeth and Anita G. Cook
2001 *Ritual Sacrifice in Ancient Peru: New Discoveries and Interpretations.* Austin: University of Texas Press.

Berrin, Kathleen and Esther Pasztory, eds.
1993 *Teotihuacan: City of the Gods.* New York: Thames and Hudson.

Boone, Elizabeth
1995 *The Aztec World.* Washington, D.C.: Smithsonian Institution Press.

Burger, Richard
1992 *Chavín and the Origins of Andean Civilization.* New York: Thames and Hudson.

Coe, Michael
1993 *Mexico: From the Olmecs to the Aztecs,* 4th edition. New York: Thames and Hudson.

1999 *The Maya,* 6th edition. New York: Thames and Hudson.

Detroit Institute of Arts
1981 *Between Continents/Between Seas: Precolumbian Art of Costa Rica.* New York: Harry N. Abrams, Inc.

Donnan, Christopher
1994 *Ceramics of Ancient Peru.* Los Angeles: Fowler Museum of Cultural History, University of California.

2001 "Moche Ceramic Portraits." *Studies in the History of Art* 63: *Moche Art and Archaeology in Ancient Peru.* Washington, D.C.: The National Gallery.

Donnan, Christopher and Donna McClelland
1999 *Moche Fineline Painting: Its Evolution and Its Artists.* Los Angeles: Fowler Museum of Cultural History, University of California.

Fash, William
2001 *Scribes, Warriors and Kings: The City of Copan and the Ancient Maya,* revised edition. New York: Thames and Hudson.

Grieder, Terence
1978 *The Art and Archaeology of Pashash.* Austin: University of Texas Press.

Hearne, Pamela and Robert J. Sharer, eds.
1992 *River of Gold: Precolumbian Treasures from Sitio Conte.* Philadelphia: The University Museum of Archaeology and Anthropology.

Helms, Mary
2000 *The Curassow's Crest: Myths and Symbols in the Ceramics of Ancient Panama.* Gainesville: University of Florida Press.

Jones, Julie, ed.
1998 *Jade in Ancient Costa Rica.* New York: The Metropolitan Museum of Art.

King, Heidi
1999 *Rain of the Moon: Silver in Ancient Peru.* New York: The Metropolitan Museum of Art.

Kolata, Alan
1995 *The Tiwanaku: Portrait of an Andean Civilization.* London: Blackwell Publishers.

Labbé, Armand
1995 *Guardians of the Life Stream: Shamans, Art and Power in Prehispanic Central Panamá.* Santa Ana, Calif.: The Bowers Museum of Cultural Art.

1998 *Shamans, Gods, and Mythic Beasts: Colombian Gold and Ceramics in Antiquity.* New York: American Federation of Arts.

Marcus, Joyce and Kent V. Flannery
1996 *Zapotec Civilization: How Urban Society Evolved in Mexico's Oaxaca Valley.* New York: Thames and Hudson.

Martin, Simon and Nikolai Grube
2000 *Chronicle of the Maya Kings and Queens: Deciphering the Dynasties of the Ancient Maya.* New York: Thames and Hudson.

The Metropolitan Museum of Art
1985 *The Art of Precolumbian Gold: The Jan Mitchell Collection.* New York.

Miller, Mary
1986 *The Art of Mesoamerica from Olmec to Aztec.* New York: Thames and Hudson.

1999 *Maya Art and Architecture.* New York: Thames and Hudson.

Morris, Craig and Adriana von Hagen
1996 *The Inka Empire and Its Andean Origins.* New York: Abbeville Press Publishers.

Moseley, Michael
2000 *The Incas and Their Ancestors: The Archaeology of Peru,* revised edition. New York: Thames and Hudson.

Pollard, Helen P.
1993 *Taríacuri's Legacy: The Prehispanic Tarascan State.* Norman: The University of Oklahoma Press.

Reents-Budet, Dorie
1994 *Painting the Maya Universe: Royal Ceramics of the Classic Period.* Winston-Salem, N.C.: Duke University Press.

Richardson, James
1994 *People of the Andes.* Washington, D.C.: Smithsonian Institution Press.

Silverman, Helaine and Donald A. Proulx
2002 *The Nasca.* Malden, Mass.: Blackwell Publishers.

Stone-Miller, Rebecca
1994 *To Weave for the Sun: Ancient Andean Textiles.* New York: Thames and Hudson.

1996 *Art of the Andes: From Chavín to Inca.* New York: Thames and Hudson.

Townsend, Richard F.
1992 *The Ancient Americas: Art from Ancient Landscapes.* Munich: Prestel Verlag.

1992 *The Aztecs.* New York: Thames and Hudson.

1998 *Ancient West Mexico: Art and Archaeology of the Unknown Past.* New York: Thames and Hudson.